BABE DIDRIKSON ZAHARIAS

by

William R. Sanford

&

Carl R. Green

CRESTWOOD HOUSE

New York

Maxwell Macmillan Canada
Toronto

Maxwell Macmillan International
New York Oxford Singapore Sydney

Library of Congress Cataloging-in-Publication Data
Sanford, William R. (William Reynolds), 1927–
  Babe Didrikson Zaharias / by William R. Sanford and Carl R. Green. — 1st ed.
    p. cm. — (Sports immortals)
  Includes bibliographical references and index.
  Summary: A biography of the female athlete who broke records in golf, track and field and a variety of other sports.
  ISBN 0-89686-736-6
    1. Zaharias, Babe Didrikson, 1911–1956—Juvenile literature. 2. Athletes—United States—Biography—Juvenile literature.
3. Women athletes—United States—Biography—Juvenile literature. [1. Zaharias, Babe Didrikson, 1911–1956. 2. Athletes.]
I. Green, Carl R. II. Title. III. Series.
GV697.Z26S26   1993
796'.092—dc20
[B]   91-44870

Photo Credits
All photos courtesy of the Bettmann Archive

CRESTWOOD HOUSE

Macmillan Publishing Company
866 Third Avenue
New York, NY 10022

Maxwell Macmillan Canada, Inc.
1200 Eglinton Avenue East
Suite 200
Don Mills, Ontario M3C 3N1

Macmillan Publishing Company is part of the Maxwell Communication Group of Companies.

Produced by Flying Fish Studio

Printed in the United States of America

First edition

10 9 8 7 6 5 4 3 2 1

CONTENTS

Sports legend, Babe Didrikson Zaharias

A One-Woman Track Team

Dyche Stadium in Evanston, Illinois was packed with excited track fans on July 16, 1932. The meet was a big one—the National Women's Track and Field Championship. But 1932 was also an Olympic year. Winners would go on to represent the United States at the Olympic Games in Los Angeles.

The crowd buzzed and cheered as each team was introduced. At last the announcer called out, "The Golden Cyclones, from Dallas, Texas!" The cheers became a roar as a slender young woman ran onto the field. No one ran with her. Mildred (Babe) Didrikson was a one-woman track team.

Babe was entered in eight of the meet's ten events. "It was one of those days in an athlete's life when you know you're just right," she wrote later. "You feel you could fly. . . . For two and a half hours, I was flying all over the place. I'd run a **heat** in the 80-meter hurdles, and then I'd take one of my high jumps. Then I'd go over to the broad jump and take a turn at that."

5

Almost everything Babe touched turned to gold. She won the shot put with a world-record throw of 39 feet 6¼ inches. A second world record fell in Babe's favorite running event, the 80-meter hurdles. She won her heat in a blazing 11.9 seconds. Later in the day she came back to win the finals in 12.1 seconds.

Babe already owned the world record in the javelin. On this day of days she broke that record and set another in the baseball throw. In the high jump she tied for first—with a world-record jump of 5 feet 3³/₁₆ inches. After that she went on to win the long jump and place fourth in the discus throw. The 100-yard dash was the only event in which she failed to score.

Now it was time to count up the team scores. The 22-member Illinois Women's Athletic Club had earned 22 points. But Babe, the one-woman team, had scored 30! All by herself, the 21-year-old had won the national championship. Reporters ran to file stories about the "wonder girl."

George Kirksey wrote that Babe's big day was "the most amazing series of performances . . . in track history." For her part, Babe was still full of energy. She went out with friends and danced until 3:00 A.M. Then she bounced up the next day and went back to the track for a workout. "I wanted to make sure my muscles didn't tighten up or anything," she said.

Babe had a promise to keep. As a child, she had told her father that she would someday win an Olympic gold medal. Now she had a chance to make good on that childish boast.

TRIVIA 1* From whom did Babe think she inherited her incredible athletic talent?

* Answers to all Trivia Quiz questions can be found on page 47.

The javelin throw was one of Babe's top track and field events.

A TOMBOY GROWS UP

In 1901 a Norwegian ship dropped anchor near Port Arthur, Texas. Thanks to the new Spindletop oil field, the region was booming. Ole Didriksen, the ship's carpenter, surveyed the busy scene and liked what he saw. Back in Norway, he told his wife, Hannah, that their lives would be better if they emigrated to America.

Because money was tight, the Didriksens moved in stages. Ole came first, finding work as a carpenter and saving his paychecks. Three years later Hannah arrived with the couple's three children. By then Ole had bought a piece of land in Port Arthur. On it he built a snug wooden house. Hannah gave birth to twins Lillie and Louis a year after she arrived.

The family felt safe in the little house. A sixth child, Mildred Ella, was born on June 26, 1911. No one thought of her as "Babe" in those days. Disaster struck when she was four. A few hours after her brother Arthur was born in 1915, a hurricane hit Port Arthur. Lillie later wrote, "Everything was gone in the flood. Ducks, chickens, trees, beds, money, dishes, everything." Ole was forced to move his family to Beaumont, 17 miles away.

Mildred grew up on Doucette Street, near the Magnolia Oil Refinery. It was a tough part of town. To make ends meet, Ole

 TRIVIA 2 Although Babe is best remembered as a world-class golfer, she first gained fame as a basketball player. How many times was she named to All-American teams when she played with the Golden Cyclones?

went back to sea and Hannah took in laundry. When she was old enough, Mildred worked after school. She earned 30 cents an hour packing figs and 67 cents an hour sewing burlap bags. Most of the money went to Hannah to help stretch the family budget.

Ole built a gym set in the backyard. He believed exercise would help children grow tall and healthy. The barbells were broomsticks with flatirons tied to each end. The makeshift gym suited Mildred, who loved active sports. It did not bother her to be called a tomboy.

"I've competed against boys as long as I can remember," she wrote later. "If a girl wants to become an athlete and do some winning, that's what she has to do. Play against the boys, get smashed around. . . . I've done some smashing of my own." In high school she floored a big football player with a right to the chin.

Mildred loved a challenge. Instead of running down the street like her friends, she hurdled the hedges between the yards. Baseball was one of her favorite sports. She hit long home runs like the great baseball star, Babe Ruth. To her delight, her friends began calling her Babe. (Years later, she also changed the spelling of her family name, from Didriksen to Didrikson.)

Babe grew up slim and straight and strong. She took pride in her strength and speed, not her looks. Hair was something to be cut short and makeup was a nuisance. When she was not wearing overalls and a T-shirt, she pulled on a shapeless cotton dress. When she relaxed a warm smile softened her sharp features. Her friends said her clear gray-green eyes were her best feature.

At home Hannah made sure that her daughters knew how to cook, clean and sew. At school Babe earned good grades in class. But most of her energy went into sports. In high school she competed in women's basketball, baseball, golf, tennis, volley-ball and swimming. As a junior, she made the All-State squad in basketball. She wanted to play football, but the school would not let her compete against boys.

Babe did not need any career counseling. "I knew exactly what I wanted to be when I grew up," she wrote in 1955. "My goal was to be the greatest athlete that ever lived."

STARRING FOR THE GOLDEN CYCLONES

With Babe as its star the Beaumont High School women's basketball team, the Miss Royal Purples, never lost a game. In early 1930 the Miss Royal Purples met Houston in a big game. Colonel Melvin J. McCombs was watching from the stands. McCombs ran the sports program of the Employers Casualty Insurance Company in Dallas. He was scouting players for his women's basketball team, the Golden Cyclones.

Babe scored 26 points that night, catching McCombs's eye with her hard-nosed style. After the game he offered her a job. For Babe this was a dream come true. She would work during the day as a typist and play basketball at night. The salary of $75 a month also sounded good. She would be making more money than most of the men she knew.

At first, Ole and Hannah said no. Taking the job would mean dropping out of school and leaving home. But Babe pleaded that this was her big chance. Ole thought it over and changed his mind. Babe promised to return to graduate with her class.

In Dallas Babe lived on a budget. She spent $5 a month for a room and 50 cents a day for breakfast and dinner. Driving to work with Colonel McCombs saved bus fare. At the office she worked hard to improve her typing skills. Soon she was keeping up with the other typists. On payday she mailed $40 home to her parents.

When the office closed, Babe worked out with the Golden Cyclones. In her first game, she played against the national champs from Sun Oil. Opposing players banged her around, but Babe kept her eye on the basket. In a 48–18 win she scored more points than the combined Sun Oil team. Sun Oil gained some revenge in the **Amateur Athletic Union's** national play-offs. Despite Babe's fine play, the Cyclones lost the title game by a single point.

The Cyclones competed in a number of sports. When the basketball season ended the women moved on to swimming, baseball and tennis. Babe loved "fancy diving" and hoped to compete in the Olympics as a diver. But McCombs had other ideas. He started his soon-to-be-famous one-woman track team.

Track workouts helped Babe mature physically. She grew to five feet seven inches and filled out to 115 pounds. Like all athletes, she was proud of her lean, muscular body. Running, jumping and throwing came naturally to her. After supper, she built up stamina by running the Haines Street hill.

Did Babe ever try a sport at which she did not excel?

In May 1930 Babe competed in her first track meet. She entered four events and won them all. A month later she picked up more medals at the southern AAU meet. Then she had the medals made into a bracelet. "Look," she said proudly, "all gold, no silver."

Babe led the Cyclones to a national basketball title in 1931. In those low-scoring days, she averaged an astounding 33 points a game. That summer she competed in the national AAU track meet in Jersey City. Afterward, a local paper called her "the world's outstanding all-round female athlete." Babe had won medals in the baseball throw, the 80-meter hurdles and the long jump.

Babe won more fans than friends. Some of her own teammates disliked her. They said she bragged too much and used rough language. Others complained that she played only for her own glory. Babe ignored the criticism. She came back in 1932 and led the Cyclones to a second championship. Then, in July, she put on her one-woman track show at the AAU national finals. Her six gold medals guaranteed her a place on the U.S. Olympic team.

TAKING THE OLYMPICS BY STORM

In 1932 the **Great Depression** held the United States tightly in its grip. Banks were failing and jobs were scarce. In those dark times Americans welcomed the excitement of the Olympic Games. That summer 2,000 athletes gathered in Los Angeles to compete for Olympic gold.

After her triumph at the AAU finals, Babe was a star attraction. Reporters wrote about the wind sprints she ran in the aisles of the train. Photographers took shots of her joking with Clark

Gable and Will Rogers. Papers all over the country printed her Texas-sized boast. "I am out to beat everybody in sight," she said, "and that's just what I'm going to do!"

Babe lived up to her word in the 1932 Olympics. She is shown here after setting the world's record in the javelin throw.

The Olympics opened on August 1. Over 100,000 people filled the newly built coliseum. Cannons roared, bands blared march tunes and pigeons flew skyward. Babe wobbled on her new high heels as she marched with the U.S. team. As the speeches droned on and on, her feet hurt more and more. At last she kicked off the tight shoes. The other women soon followed her lead.

Olympic rules limited women to no more than three events. The U.S. team entered Babe in the 80-meter hurdles, the high jump and the javelin throw. During workouts a coach tried to change her hurdling style. Babe told him that she had learned to hurdle by jumping hedges. "I'm not about to change now," she said.

The javelin throw was held late on the second day. Because the field was crowded with athletes Babe could not warm up properly. Then, when her turn came, her hand slipped as she started her run. Without breaking stride she regripped the shaft and hurled the javelin 143 feet 4 inches. The arrowlike throw broke the old world record by 11 feet. The awkward motion also injured her right shoulder. Babe ignored the pain.

Two days later Babe set a world record in her heat of the 80-meter hurdles. Her teammate Evelyne Hall matched Babe's time in winning her own heat. That set up a final race that matched Evelyne's graceful style against Babe's power. When the race started, Babe was slow in leaving the starting line. With the crowd roaring she chased Evelyne for 80 meters—and caught her at the tape. The margin was razor-thin, but the judges declared Babe the winner, finishing in 11.7 seconds.

Could Babe become the first woman to win three gold medals? "Watch me," Babe said. In the high jump finals, Babe and Jean

The winners of the 1932 Olympics 80-meter women's hurdle event. Gold-medal-winner Babe Didrikson stands between silver-medal-winner Evelyne Hall on her left and bronze-medal-winner Marjorie Clark of South Africa, on her right.

Shiley both cleared 5 feet 5 inches. The height was a new world record. In a jump-off, Jean missed at 5 feet 5³/₄ inches. Babe cleared the bar—but hit the upright as she landed. The bar teetered and fell into the pit.

Now the height was brought back to 5 feet 5 inches. Both women soared over the bar—but then the judges took a stand. They said that Babe's head had cleared the bar before her body. Her jump would be legal today, but in 1932 it was ruled an illegal dive. Babe had to settle for the silver medal.

Babe complained that she had always jumped that way. But she calmed down and accepted her medal. When the Olympics ended sportswriters named her the top athlete of the games. She returned to Dallas, where the city held a parade in her honor. Babe rode in the fire chief's open car, waving to the crowd through a blizzard of confetti.

A few months later the Associated Press named her Woman Athlete of the Year. Babe felt as if she were on top of the world.

Babe poses with members of her proud family after her Olympic victories. From left to right: Lillie, Ole, Babe and Hannah.

ANYTHING TO MAKE A BUCK

Babe's Olympic victories made her a public figure. Rumors about her future spread quickly. One story said she planned to swim the English Channel. Another said she was training to fight bulls in Mexico. A third claimed that she would soon be modeling clothes in London. None of the stories was true.

If Babe hoped to cash in on her fame, she was let down. With no firm contracts in hand she was forced to return to her old job. Only when an Illinois firm offered $300 a month did Employers Casualty give her a raise. For a time Babe felt almost rich. She purchased clothes, a stove and an icebox for her family.

In late 1932 Babe bought a red Dodge coupe. A few weeks later the company featured her in its ads. The AAU assumed Babe was being paid for the ads and took away her **amateur-athlete** standing. That was a crushing blow, for it meant she could no longer play for the Golden Cyclones. An angry Babe argued that Dodge had run the ads without her approval. When the company confirmed her statement, the AAU withdrew its ruling.

With the battle won, Babe had second thoughts. She knew that Olympic fame fades quickly. Why not use her public image to make some money? A few days later she signed a contract with Chrysler. The company assigned her to appear at the Detroit auto show. With Babe on duty, there was always a crowd around the Dodge display.

TRIVIA 4

Babe set a world record for the javelin by throwing 143 feet 4 inches at the 1932 Olympics. How does that throw compare to today's world record?

17

Although the Olympics were over, Babe continued to stay in top physical form. She is shown here during a training session in a New York gym.

When the show ended Babe hired George Emerson to find more work. Emerson signed her to do a vaudeville show in Chicago. For $2,500 a week Babe told jokes, jogged on a treadmill, sang and played the harmonica. To end the show, she drove plastic golf balls into the audience. It was not much of an act, but Babe's fans packed the theater.

Despite her success Babe missed athletics. She told Emerson to find jobs that used her sports skills. Soon she was playing basketball for the Brooklyn Yankees. In a rough-and-tumble game, she tossed in 9 of her team's 19 points. Since the other team only scored 16, that was enough to win. Babe earned $400 and some painful bruises for her night's work.

Babe shoots for the basket during a practice session with the Brooklyn Yankees.

Now Babe was hitting her stride. She put a basketball team together called Babe Didrikson's All-Americans. The four men and three women played men's teams around the Midwest. They won most of their games and drew good crowds. Babe cleared $2,000 a month.

In 1934 Babe turned to her old love, baseball. During spring training, teams paid her $200 for each inning she pitched. Babe had good control, but she did not have a major-league fastball. In one game only a triple play ended the first inning without a run scoring.

Before long Babe was pitching for the all-male House of David team. Fans teased her for being the only player who did not wear a full beard. Like the All-Americans, the House of David moved from town to town, playing local teams. In Chicago Babe hit a home run to win her own game, 1–0. She played in 200 games, driving her own car from one town to the next.

The gypsy life grew tiresome. Babe also worried about the future. Playing men's baseball made her something of a freak. Shooting pool or putting on boxing **exhibitions** was no better. It was time to find a sport she could play for years to come.

TRIVIA 5

All of Babe's track and field records have been broken but one. Which record does she still hold?

Babe enjoyed all athletic competition. She is shown here sparring with boxing instructor Bryan Hayes.

BABE TURNS TO GOLF

Babe resigned from the House of David team at the end of the 1934 season. Too many people were laughing at the "wonder girl" who competed against men. This was an age when men thought women should be dainty and shy. Babe refused to play that game. She said shy, dainty women were "sissies."

For a while Babe thought tennis would serve her purpose. She threw herself into the game, attacking the ball with sharp, crisp ground strokes. But the shoulder she had hurt in the Olympics was not fully healed. Raising her arm to serve the ball became more and more painful. The pain forced Babe to give up on tennis.

Babe charged full speed into tennis as she did with every sport she tried.

At this low point in Babe's career, the golfer Bobby Jones played an exhibition in Houston. Babe followed the world champion around the course, watching every move he made. She liked the way he stepped up to the **tee** and "slugged the ball." Rain cut the match short but Babe had seen enough. This was her game!

To pay the bills while she improved her golf, Babe went back to her old job. Her boss helped by paying her fees at a local country club. The **club pro** gave her lessons. Soon Babe was playing well enough to enter her first tournament.

The Fort Worth Women's Invitational was held in November 1934. Before the **qualifying round** Babe told a reporter she would shoot a 77. Then she went out and shot exactly that, a 77. When **match play** started Babe lost in the first round. That was a letdown, but she did not mope about her loss. Instead, she set her sights on the 1935 Texas Women's Amateur Championship.

Life settled into a routine. Babe arrived at the golf course at dawn each day, ready for three hours of practice. Then she raced to her job at the insurance company. During the lunch hour she practiced putting on the carpet in her boss's office. After work she returned to the course for more lessons.

In April Babe practiced for a week at the River Oaks Country Club. After qualifying with an 84, she started match play. In match play each hole counts as one point. A golfer must win ten holes out of 18 to advance to the next round. Babe cruised into the **semifinals** by winning her first three matches.

The semifinal match was tougher. On a rainy day, Babe was tied with R. E. Winger going into the last hole. Both women reached the green in three. Winger's putt hung on the lip of the hole and refused to drop. Babe then faced her own long putt across a soggy green. She stroked the ball solidly and watched as it plowed toward the hole. The ball seemed to stop—and then it dropped in. Babe raised her arms in triumph.

The finals pitted Babe against Texas champion Peggy Chandler. At the halfway point of the 36-hole match, Babe trailed by a single hole. At last, on the 30th hole, she drew even with Chandler. Four holes later, Babe found her second shot lying in a water-filled rut. She took a sand wedge and blasted the ball toward the green. It bounced, rolled and fell into the cup for an **eagle**. Although the miracle shot gave Babe the lead, Chandler rallied to tie the match. But Babe was not to be denied. She **birdied** the final hole to win her first championship.

Babe set her sights on winning the national amateur title. In those days, however, golf was ruled by the country-club set. Snooty society women said Babe was "too loud and too common." The U.S. Golf Association (USGA) backed them up. A ruling was issued that said Babe could no longer play in amateur tournaments. Her crime? She had played baseball and basketball for money.

BABE FINDS A PARTNER

Despite widespread protests, the USGA refused to change its ruling. If Babe wanted to play tournament golf, she would have to play in **open tournaments**. These tournaments allowed **pros** and amateurs to compete against each other. But only one tournament—the Western Open—allowed female pros to compete.

Since the USGA said she was a pro, Babe decided to make some "do-re-me." She signed a contract for $5,000 a year to

endorse Wilson golf clubs. Then she went on tour with Gene Sarazen, a top male golfer. She earned $150 for each exhibition she played with him. Sarazen was a long hitter, but Babe sometimes outdrove him. Her longest drives measured over 300 yards.

Babe still thought women's fashions were silly, but she had learned the value of looking good. Bertha Bowen, a close friend, helped her choose more stylish clothes. Babe let her hair grow and learned to use makeup. For the first time writers began to describe her as pretty.

The lack of tournament play did not stop Babe from working overtime. She moved to Los Angeles and then to Illinois. At each stop she took lessons and practiced until her hands bled. Tommy Armour, a great teacher, helped straighten out her booming drives.

In January 1938 Babe entered the Los Angeles Open. That raised a few golfing eyebrows. No women had ever played in this men's open. Still, there was no rule barring them. Babe and Alice Bauer promptly shot their way into the tournament.

Babe met her partners when she went to the tee for her first round. One was a church minister. The other was a handsome wrestler named George Zaharias. On posters he was billed as THE CRYING GREEK FROM CRIPPLE CREEK. In the dramas played out in wrestling rings, George was cast as the bad guy. Wrestling fans loved to boo him, but he was really a kind, gentle person. He also had a good head for business.

TRIVIA 6

Babe pitched for a legendary baseball player when she toured with the House of David baseball team. Who was the team's manager in 1934?

Before the threesome teed off, Babe and George clowned for the news cameras. George reached out and pulled Babe into a headlock. Babe loved it. Perhaps her mind was not on her golf after that. Both Babe and George failed to make the cut. Neither seemed to care. That night George asked her to go dancing. Before long she was taking him to meet her mother.

A few weeks later Babe left Los Angeles to drive her mother and sister to Beaumont. By the time she reached Phoenix she knew she belonged with George. After putting her mother and sister on a train Babe drove back to Los Angeles. There she learned that George was wrestling in San Francisco. Babe picked up George's brother for company and headed north that same night. When George opened his door to her knock he smiled and said, "Come here, Romance."

Six months later George gave Babe an engagement ring. But both athletes lived busy lives. George wrestled most nights and Babe played in any tournament that would have her. Wedding dates were set and then broken. At last George roared, "We're going to get married this week or we call off the deal."

Babe did not hesitate. "The deal's on," she said. She married George in St. Louis two days before Christmas 1938. But schedules still had to be kept. George did not take his bride on a honeymoon—to Australia—until four months later.

TRIVIA 7

Today a top woman golfer may win ten or 20 tournaments in her career. How many tournaments did Babe win during her lifetime?

BABE HITS HER GOLFING PEAK

Babe—now Babe Didrikson Zaharias—came back from her honeymoon in high spirits. Australia's sports fans had fallen in love with her. With George as her manager, she looked for new golfing worlds to conquer. But Babe was still banned from most pro tournaments because she was a female. Until that barrier fell, she was limited to playing in open tournaments.

An odd clause in the USGA rule book opened the gate. A pro who went three years without playing for money could become an amateur again. Luckily, Babe could afford the loss of income. George was already a millionaire. In 1940 Babe played in two open tournaments. She won the Texas Women's Open and the Western Women's Open. True to her vow, she refused the prize money.

Babe liked to cook, sew and garden, but home arts soon bored her. After she and George settled in Los Angeles, Babe took up tennis again. Anxious to perfect her game, she sometimes played 17 sets a day. By 1941 she felt ready for tournament play, but amateur tennis was more rigid than golf. The rule was clear: "Once a pro, always a pro."

Sports were no fun for Babe if she could not compete for prizes. She threw down her tennis racquet and picked up a bowling ball. At first she used brute strength to speed the ball straight down the alley. Then she mastered the higher-scoring hook shot. Before long she was bringing bowling trophies home by the arm load.

On December 7, 1941 the Japanese attacked Pearl Harbor. With the nation at war, George tried to enlist. He was turned down because of **varicose veins**. Babe did her part by helping with the sale of war bonds. To attract crowds, she golfed with the movie stars Bob Hope and Bing Crosby. After playing with Babe, Hope joked, "There's only one thing wrong about Babe and me. I hit the ball like a girl and she hits like a man."

Golf fans loved her wisecracks and trick shots. To show off, Babe liked to tee up five golf balls in a line. Then, using her driver she hit each one high and far. The first ball would still be in the air when she hit the last one.

The USGA welcomed Babe back to amateur standing in 1944. Now 32, she signed up to play in a charity match at Palm Springs. Once again the "wonder girl" made headlines. Babe smashed the Desert Golf Club record by shooting a 137 for 36 holes.

In 1944 Babe stepped up to the major tournaments. She had won the Western Women's Open as a pro four years earlier. Now she won it again as an amateur. After she repeated her victory in 1945 she was named Woman Athlete of the Year. Babe was happy to be back on top, but it was a sad time too. Her mother had died during the tournament.

National tournaments were suspended during WWII, but when the war ended in 1945, Babe was free to enter tournament after tournament. From her new home in Colorado, she raced from one match to the next. Her game seemed to grow stronger with each outing. During mid-1940s, she won 17 major women's golf tournaments in a row. Then she traveled to Scotland to play in the 1947 British Women's Amateur. In the finals, despite rain and a sore thumb, Babe became the first woman from the United States to win this tournament. She danced a joyous Highland fling while the Scots cheered the "world's greatest woman golfer."

Babe Didrikson Zaharias takes a swing during the Western Women's Open.

BIRTH OF THE WOMEN'S PRO TOUR

Denver gave Babe a huge key to the city when she came back from Scotland. Two weeks later she won the Broadmoor Match Play Tournament. Promoters hurried to wave big money offers at her. As long as Babe was an amateur she had to turn them down.

At last the lure of easy money became too great. Babe signed with a top sports agent and told the press that she was turning pro again in August 1947. When reporters crowded around, she said she planned to play in the U.S. Open—against men. The USGA did not think that was funny. Officials quickly passed a rule against women playing in the men's open.

The new rule may have hurt Babe's pride but it did not hurt her bank account. She was soon earning $100,000 a year from endorsements and exhibitions. Taking a page from the past, she put on her baseball uniform again. In a practice game she struck out the great Joe DiMaggio. Babe also played in charity golf matches with the rich and famous. Future President Dwight D. Eisenhower asked her for tips on improving his own game.

In 1948 Babe was the top money winner in women's golf—but she took home only $3,400. Purses were small and tournaments were few and far between. The men's pro tour was growing, Babe saw, because the men were better organized. In January 1949 she helped to found the Ladies Professional Golf Association (LPGA). Wilson Sporting Goods put up the first $15,000 in prizes.

Baseball legend Babe Ruth gets pitching tips from another famous Babe— all-around athlete Babe Didrikson Zaharias.

With Babe leading the way, the LPGA was an instant success. The first year's roster of six women pros soon grew to 30. Within four years, LPGA members were competing in over 20 tournaments. Prize money grew just as quickly, to $225,000. Once again, Babe was the top money winner. Some of her fellow golfers envied her success as much as they disliked her brash style. In the locker room, Babe was likely to yell, "Babe's here! Now who's gonna finish second?"

More honors came Babe's way. In 1950 she was named the Outstanding Woman Athlete of the Half Century. That raised her to the level of Babe Ruth, Jim Thorpe and other sports immortals. Next, Chicago's Sky Crest Country Club hired her as its teaching pro. Babe relished the honor of being the first woman to hold the job. Even though she often left to play in tournaments, Babe gave the club its money's worth. She put in long hours giving lessons.

Babe turned forty in 1951. That year George bought a country club in Tampa, Florida. When they were home the couple lived in a house on the club grounds. Fixed up and renamed the Tampa Golf and Country Club, the course was soon making money. Babe's name brought in many new members.

The years 1950 and 1951 were two of Babe's best. She topped the list of money winners with totals of $13,550 and $15,087. To reach those totals, she had to win most of the big women's tournaments. When she did not win, she could be counted on to finish second or third.

Babe started 1952 as if nothing could stop her. She won the Women's Titleholders in March. By April she was again the top money winner. But then she faltered. For the first time in 40 years, her athlete's body was failing her.

Babe displayed her great skill in golf in almost every tournament she played in.

BABE LOSES A MATCH WITH CANCER

As early as 1948 Babe had suffered from a swelling in her back. As with most of her injuries, she tried to ignore the pain. A hot bath and a good night's sleep seemed to help. But the pain grew worse, not better. By 1952 Babe was feeling faint.

George nagged his wife into visiting her family doctor. Dr. Tatum found a damaged artery in her leg. A blockage there could have killed her. After surgery, Babe snapped back quickly. Six months later she won the Texas Women's Open.

Babe's personal life was also going through some rough times. Although she did not divorce him, Babe no longer felt close to George. In private she accused him of trying to control her life. In public the couple pretended that all was well. A second problem centered on George's eating and drinking habits. Always a big man, he ballooned to over 300 pounds.

As her marriage soured Babe found a new friend in young Betty Dodd. The two met in Tampa and were soon spending much of their time together. Babe and Betty shared the same interests, from golf to music. During matches Babe sometimes played the harmonica while Betty strummed along on the guitar. The music pleased their fans but upset their opponents.

TRIVIA 8

How many times was Babe named Woman Athlete of the Year?

Babe raises her arms victoriously after winning another pro-golf tournament.

35

For a time Babe seemed her old self. Then, in April 1953 she felt weak again. Dr. Tatum checked her leg and found that it had healed well. As he probed further, his smile faded. He told Babe she had to go to Fort Worth for more tests. Newspapers picked up the story and printed guesses about the nature of her illness.

The doctor confirmed Babe's worst fears. She had cancer. Part of her intestine would have to be cut away. Babe said the news hit her like a "thunderbolt." She and George both cried as they left the doctor's office.

Newspapers headlined the sad news. Doctors were quoted as saying Babe would never play golf again. She responded bravely to the challenge. Waking up after the operation, Babe asked for her golf clubs. Knowing her wishes, George had left them in her room. Ten days later she was back on her feet.

Babe felt a little stronger each day. At home in Tampa she was soon able to play a few holes. Fourteen weeks after her surgery she entered the All-American Open. Being Babe, she was displeased with her 15th-place finish.

A week later Babe played in the World Golf Championship. Less worried now about injuring herself, she finished third. But could she win again? Babe soon answered that question. In February 1954 she made her comeback official by winning the Women's Open. But George was holding something back. The doctors had told him the cancer had spread to Babe's lymph nodes. There was little the medicine of the day could do for her.

George Zaharias watches his wife in practice as she tries to make a comeback after her cancer surgery.

Babe kept on playing—and winning. In 1954 she entered 18 tournaments and won five of them. She came in second or third in seven more. But winning did not erase the pain in her back. In early 1955 doctors operated to repair a ruptured disc. By now the cancer had reached her lower spine. The pain did not go away.

Babe was in and out of hospitals after that. X-ray treatments did not help. In the summer of 1956 she went into the hospital for the last time. Doctors tried to ease her pain, but with little success. On September 27 she looked at George and whispered, "I ain't gonna die, honey."

Three hours later Babe Didrikson Zaharias broke that promise. The great athlete was only 45 years old when she died.

TRIVIA 9 How much money did Babe make when she won her record 17 tournaments in a row?

Babe blows out her birthday candles during the surprise party in her hospital room thrown by her husband George.

BABE DIDRIKSON ZAHARIAS, SPORTS IMMORTAL

The nation mourned Babe's death. President Eisenhower paid tribute to his golfing friend. He said, "She was a woman who in her athletic career certainly won the admiration of every person in the United States."

Babe would have been pleased by those kind words. Perhaps she would have liked Patty Berg's comments even more. Berg, an old friend and fellow golfer, was a cofounder of the LPGA. She said, "Our sport grew because of Babe, because she had so much flair and color. With Babe there was never a dull moment."

Babe's friends and fans did not forget her. The John Healy Hospital in Galveston, Texas set up a cancer fund in her name. The Babe Didrikson Zaharias Trophy was created to honor the year's best woman athlete. Her hometown of Beaumont raised funds to build the Babe Didrikson Zaharias Museum. The circular building houses her trophies, medals, golf clubs and other treasures.

The passing years have not dimmed her memory. In 1975 the Babe Didrikson Zaharias Foundation held a fund-raising event in her honor. The dinner featured the first showing of *Babe*, a film about her life. Six years later the U.S. Postal Service issued a stamp in Babe's honor. It showed a grinning Babe holding a huge silver trophy.

TRIVIA 10

Babe won the 1954 U.S. Women's Open by 12 strokes, a margin of victory that has been equaled but never exceeded. Why did her fans say the victory was so special?

Babe Didrikson Zaharias was the first three-time winner of the U.S. Women's Open Golf Championship.

Sports immortal Babe Didrikson Zaharias during a 1933 workout session

During Babe's lifetime some women golfers accused her of being brash and self-centered. Perhaps there is some truth in the charges. What those critics forgot was that Babe made their sport possible. The headlines she earned brought new money and public acceptance to women's golf. When Babe was a top money winner in 1954 her paychecks totaled only $12,112. Thanks to the doors she opened, purses grew larger year by year. Today's top money winners take home $600,000 or more a year.

Babe's influence did not stop with women's golf. In 1932 one writer described her as "the muscle moll to end all muscle molls." Strong, athletic women drew sneers instead of praise. But over the years Americans learned to honor Babe's athletic talent. Today, muscles and athletic talents are "in."

Many children dream of growing up to be "the greatest." Babe was lucky enough to see her dreams come true. Along the way she also learned that gold medals are not everything. "Winning has always meant so much to me . . . ," she wrote near the end of her life. Then she added, "but winning friends has meant the most."

GLOSSARY

amateur athlete—Someone who competes for the love of sport, not for money.

Amateur Athletic Union (AAU)—In Babe's day, the AAU was the governing body for amateur sport in the United States.

birdie—To finish a hole in one under par. A golfer who shoots a three on a four-par hole is credited with a birdie.

club pro—A professional golfer hired by a golf club to give lessons to the members.

eagle—To complete a hole in two strokes under par. Eagles are almost as rare as holes-in-one.

endorsement—Paying an athlete or other public figure to represent a product in hopes of increasing sales.

exhibition—An unofficial game or match played to call the public's attention to an athlete's skills.

Great Depression—The period during the 1930s when the U.S. economy collapsed and many people lost their jobs.

heat—A preliminary race held to determine the athletes who will compete in the finals.

match play—A golf tournament in which winners are decided by the number of holes they win, not by the total number of strokes. Match play was common in Babe's day, but is rare in modern golf.

open tournament—A golf tournament which is open to both amateurs and pros.

professional (pro) athlete—Someone who makes his or her living by competing in a sport.

44

qualifying round—Entrants are sometimes asked to prove their abilities by shooting a target score in a round played before the official start of a tournament.

semifinals—Winners of a semifinal match or heat qualify for the finals of a tournament or race.

tee—The grassy areas on a golf course from which players hit their first shots on each hole.

varicose veins—Enlarged blood vessels that rupture easily.

MORE GOOD READING ABOUT
BABE DIDRIKSON ZAHARIAS

Johnson, William O. and N. P. Williamson. *Whatta-gal! The Babe Didrikson Story*. Boston: Little, Brown, & Co., 1977.

Knudson, R. Rozanne. *Babe Didrikson: Athlete of the Century*. New York: Viking, 1985.

Lynn, Elizabeth. *Babe Didrikson Zaharias*. New York: Chelsea House, 1989.

Schoor, Gene. *Babe Didrikson: The World's Greatest Woman Athlete*. Garden City, N.Y.: Doubleday & Co., 1978.

Zaharias, Mildred D. *This Life I've Led: My Autobiography*. New York: A. S. Barnes, 1955.

BABE DIDRIKSON ZAHARIAS TRIVIA QUIZ

1: When she was a youth in Norway Babe's mother, Hannah, was an outstanding skier and skater. Babe believed she took after her mother when it came to athletics.

2: Babe was named to the women's All-American basketball team three times, in 1930, 1931 and 1932.

3: No. Along with basketball, golf, tennis, bowling and track, Babe excelled at sports as varied as archery, water polo, ice skating, skeetshooting, billiards and horseback riding.

4: Babe would have to improve her 1932 throw by an incredible 84 feet 1 inch to equal the current world mark. Kate Schmidt of Germany holds the record, which she set in 1977.

5: Babe still holds the record for the baseball throw at 296 feet. This event was dropped from track competition in 1957.

6: Babe's manager on the House of David team was Grover Cleveland Alexander. Alexander should have been a good judge of pitching talent. He was one of the greatest pitchers of all time.

7: During her lifetime Babe won a total of 82 tournaments, 51 amateur and 31 professional.

8: Babe was named Woman Athlete of the Year six times—in 1932, 1945, 1946, 1947, 1950 and 1954. No other athlete has won this honor so many times.

9: Babe did not make any money for winning her 17 tournaments in a row. All were amateur events.

10: Babe was still recovering from her first cancer surgery when she won the 1954 Women's Open.

Index